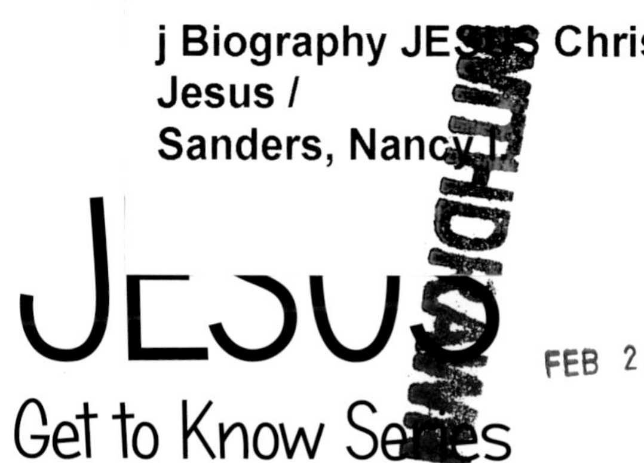

Nancy I. Sanders

JESUS

Nancy I. Sanders

ZONDERKIDZ

Jesus

This title is also available as a Zondervan ebook.
Visit www.zondervan.com/ebooks.

Requests for information should be addressed to:

Zonderkidz, 3900 *Sparks Dr., Grand Rapids, Michigan 49546*

ISBN 978-0-310-74516-7

Ronnie Ann Herman, Herman Agency

Cover design: Cindy Davis
Interior design: David Conn

Printed in China

---

14 15 16 17 18 19 DSC 20 19 18 17 16 15 14 13 12 11 10 9 8 7 6 5 4 3 2 1

Dedication

To Jon and Linda, and the next generation of believers you've raised up to be followers of the Truth.

ACKNOWLEDGMENTS

I want to thank first and foremost my husband, Jeff. As a fourth grade teacher, you always provide invaluable input into each one of my children's books, including this one! Thanks also to our wonderful sons Dan and Ben (and your new bride Christina!). Dad and I count our blessings daily because of each of you.

A special thanks goes to my dear friend Val Koukal. Thanks for stepping up to the plate and helping me with my research! I treasure your encouragement and sweet friendship.

Thanks to Ronnie Herman, my agent extraordinaire! For your help, for your guidance, for your hard work, and for your love of birds and everything green and growing. You're a treasured gem in my life!

Also a big thank you to editor Mary Hassinger, Annette Bourland, and all the amazingly wonderful folks at Zonderkidz. What an exciting journey this series has been to work on together.

Thank you to Pastor Jack and Lisa Hibbs and for your commitment to speak the truth about the Bible and the teachings of Jesus Christ. I also want to thank Charlie H. Campbell, a frequent speaker at our church and the author of reliable information about faith, history, and the Bible. May the truth taught set the record straight about the trustworthiness of the Scriptures for this generation and those to come.

TABLE OF CONTENTS

GET TO KNOW ... THIS BOOK

The Get to Know series is all about Bible heroes and the time period in which they lived. Each book in the series provides information about a person whose life and work impacts the world and Bible times. To help you understand everything in these books, we have provided features to help you recognize important information and facts.

SCRIPTURE

Look for an oil lamp to read a Scripture from the Bible.

BIBLE HERO

Look for a sandal for information about a Bible hero.

EYEWITNESS ACCOUNT

Look for a picture of an eye each time someone who saw what happened tells about it.

DID YOU KNOW?

Look for a clay jar to learn fun facts.

WORD BANK

Look for a scroll to learn the meanings of new words. The words are also in bold on the page.

Chapter 1

THE IMPORTANT PLAN

Do you know who the president of the United States is? You may have seen his photograph. You may have heard him speak on television. You may have even read a book about him. The president is very famous. It's easy to learn about his life.

But how do you learn about someone who lived long ago? Jesus is probably the most famous person who ever lived. People have heard about him. People have talked about him. People have written about him. The name of Jesus is known all over the world — more than anyone else's name in history.

Many people believe Jesus is God's Son. The people who believe this are called **Christians**. There are over

Christians: People who believe in Jesus Christ and his teachings

two billion Christians today. That is about one third of the world's population.

The problem is, Jesus lived over 2,000 years ago. There wasn't TV. There were no cameras. Nobody has ever seen his photograph. Nobody has ever heard a recording of his voice.

© Maria Dryfhout/Shutterstock

Jesus lived 2,000 years ago yet he is famous today.

So how can you learn about his life? How can you learn about the people he knew? How can you learn about the world he lived in?

One way is to look at **archaeological evidence**. Scientists called archaeologists have dug up items from

Archaeological Evidence: Objects found that show the existence of people, places, and things

Centre for Public Christianity

Archaeologists discovered this artifact on November 5, 2005. It is a mosaic floor at Megiddo. It says, "the God Jesus Christ." This mosaic was in a church about 200 years after Jesus lived.

long ago. They have found **artifacts** such as jewelry, clay jars, and furniture that, through scientific processes, have been proven to be from Jesus' time.

They study old buildings, walls, and roads. People built some of these hundreds and thousands of years

Artifacts: Objects made by people from long ago

ago. All these things are called archaeological evidence. They help us learn more about Jesus and his world.[1]

Another way to learn about Jesus is to look at documents written by people who lived around the same time Jesus did. Long ago, people carved words on rock. Others wrote on clay. Still others wrote on early kinds of paper called papyrus. These written records help us understand even more. We can learn about what people were thinking and doing around the time that Jesus lived.

We can also look at the Bible. **Bible scholars** used to question whether or not the Bible is accurate. But now many agree that new archaeological evidence helps show the Bible is a true historical document.

They show that the Bible is not made up of myths, fables, or fairy tales. The people in the Bible had a real place in history. Documents and artifacts have been found that prove they existed. The events in the Bible happened in real places that you can find on maps. You can visit many of these places today.

The Bible gives a historical account of the life and

Bible Scholars: People trained to study the Bible and its history

In 58 BC, Rome took control over the regions where the Jews lived.

Map by International Mapping.

times of Jesus. The Bible helps us understand who Jesus was.

Together, let's look at archaeological evidence, ancient historic documents, and the Bible. Together, let's learn about Jesus!

We start by looking at the world Jesus lived in. He was born a Jew. Being Jewish meant two things. One, that the person was a part of a cultural community that could trace his family origin back to the ancient Hebrew people of Israel and Abraham. And two, the person practiced Judaism as his faith.

Jesus grew up in a town called Nazareth. Nazareth was in a region called Galilee. Judea, Galilee, and Samaria were three of the regions where most Jews lived. Today, this area is the nation of Israel. During the life of Jesus, the Roman Empire ruled over this part of the world.

Jesus was born into a time of unrest. The Jews did not want the Romans to rule over them. The Romans made them pay heavy taxes. They took over their land and their soldiers marched through their streets. But worst of all, the Romans did not have the same beliefs they did.

The Jews were looking for someone to save them from the Romans. This person would be their **Messiah**. They had been waiting for the Messiah for many years.

The Jews had documents of faith called the Scriptures. The Scriptures talked about an important plan of God to send the Messiah. This plan started more than 2,500 years earlier, when God created the first people. Their names were Adam and Eve.

Sin and evil entered the perfect world God had made when Adam and Eve were tempted by the devil. But God promised Adam and Eve he would send a Messiah. The Messiah would take care of the sin problem forever.

The first great leader of the Jews was Abraham. Abraham is known as the "Father of the Jews." He believed in one God called **Yahweh**. Abraham's family were called **Hebrews**. At God's command, they moved everything they had to live in Canaan. This is where Israel is today.

Abraham believed God promised this land to his family forever. This promise was repeated to Abraham's son Isaac. Then it was repeated to his son Jacob. (God changed Jacob's name to Israel.)

In Jacob's time, there was a **famine.** Food was hard to find. Jacob's family moved to Egypt to find food. But

Messiah: The promised deliverer of the Jews

Sin: Bad things people think, say, or do

Yahweh: The Hebrew name for God

Hebrews: Another name for Jews

Famine: When no food can be found

Jacob took God's promise with him in his heart. One day God would surely bring Jacob's family back to the land he had promised to them.

Jacob's family grew bigger in Egypt. In fact, the Egyptians worried they would become too powerful. So the Egyptians made them into slaves. They were in Egypt for about 400 years.

Moses was another great leader of the Jews. Moses helped the Jews escape from Egypt and slavery. Moses led them from Egypt back to the land of Jacob. The escape from Egypt is called the **Exodus**. Every year, Jews celebrate the holiday of **Passover**. They remember the Exodus with a special meal and celebration.

He also gave them the Ten Commandments from God. These commandments are known as God's Law or the **Law of Moses**. These laws help people follow God, be kind to each other, and do good things.

The Jews eventually settled in the land of Canaan. They were now the twelve tribes of Israel and each tribe, or family, lived in its own region. Around 1000 BC they

Exodus: The escape of the Jews from Egypt

Passover: A spring Jewish holiday when the Exodus is remembered

Law of Moses: The first five books in the Bible; includes the Ten Commandments

The Ten Commandments were written on stone tablets. God gave them to Moses on the top of Mount Sinai.

Planet Art

built a central kingdom and when King David was the leader he made Jerusalem the capital city.

Over the next thousand years, there were many kings in Israel. There were wars and battles for power. There were also many **prophets**.

These prophets were holy men and women. They read the Scriptures. They studied God's Law. They told God's words to the people. The prophets spoke about the coming Messiah. Other nations conquered the nation of Israel and life was hard. They made the Jews follow their rules and the prophets worked to encourage the Jews through all of this. Then in 63 BC the Roman Empire conquered Jerusalem. The Jews groaned under their hard rule. They longed for the Messiah to come and finally set them free.

DID YOU KNOW?

Many scholars view the Bible as trustworthy. Charlie Campbell says, "There is no need to prop up a case for the reliability of the Bible on sensational finds or discoveries that are still being debated. There are a wealth of finds that have been examined and confirmed as genuine by multiple archaeological experts, both Christian and non-Christian."[2]

Prophets: People who tell God's words to others

JESUS, THE CREATOR

Paul, an early Christian leader, said, "Christ is the exact likeness of God, who can't be seen. He is first, and he is over all of creation. All things were created by him."

– Colossians 1:15–16

BIBLE HEROES

Abraham—Known as the "Father of the Jews." He lived around 2100 BC God promised the land of Israel to Abraham and his children forever.

Moses—A great leader of the Jews. He led them out of slavery in Egypt and gave them the Ten Commandments.

THE TEN COMMANDMENTS

The Bible lists the Ten Commandments in Exodus 20.[3]

1. "Do not put any other gods in place of me."
2. "Do not make statues of gods."
3. "Do not misuse the name of the Lord your God."
4. "Remember to keep the Sabbath day holy."
5. "Honor your father and mother."
6. "Do not murder."
7. "Do not commit adultery."
8. "Do not steal."
9. "Do not give false witness against your neighbor."
10. "Do not long for anything that belongs to your neighbor."

Chapter 2

A SPECIAL BIRTH

Jesus actually lived. He was a real person. Many documents show us this is true. For example, Josephus, a famous historian of Jewish and Roman history from 100 BC to 100 AD, lived around the same time as Jesus. He wrote about Jesus. Also, Jesus was friends with many people such as Matthew and John, who wrote about Jesus in the Gospels.

The **Gospels** are the first four books of the New Testament in the Bible. They are the books called Matthew, Mark, Luke, and John. All four books tell about the life of Jesus. Two of them, Matthew and Luke, also tell about his birth.

Surprising events happened when Jesus was born.

Gospel: "Good news," each of the first four books of the New Testament

Many scholars take these events very seriously. One reason is because the accounts were written by people who lived at the same time as Jesus.

The book of Matthew was written by Matthew. He was a tax collector. He became one of Jesus' **twelve disciples**. He spent three years with Jesus learning about God. Matthew later became a leader in the early church.

The book of Luke was written by Luke, a doctor. He never met Jesus but he worked with Paul. Paul was one of the early church leaders. Paul knew the twelve disciples.

Mary was the mother of Jesus. She was friends with the twelve disciples and many of Jesus' followers. She would certainly have told the disciples and others the special things that happened when Jesus was born.

We might not know how these special things happened. But just because we don't understand something, doesn't mean it's not true. For example, before scientists understood the planets and the sun, they believed the earth wasn't round.

Twelve Disciples: A special group of Jesus' closest followers

Many scholars view the Gospels as historical documents that tell us what really happened when Jesus was born. The events sound amazing. But many scholars agree they are part of history.

The Gospels say that an angel named Gabriel talked with a young Jewish woman named Mary. Gabriel said Mary was going to have a baby. This baby would be very special. First, God was his Father. He would not have a human father. Secondly, the baby would be a king. "You must name him Jesus," Gabriel told Mary.[4]

Many artists painted the meeting of Gabriel and Mary.

Wikimedia Commons

At first, Mary felt afraid. But later she shared the news with her relative Elizabeth. Elizabeth was happy for Mary. And Mary was filled with joy.

An angel also visited Joseph, the man Mary was to marry. He was told that everything was going to be fine, to trust God, and marry Mary. So Joseph and Mary were married as planned.

At that time, Rome ruled Israel. The Roman **emperor** from 31 BC to 14 AD was Caesar Augustus. He decided to count everyone living in the Roman Empire. So everyone had to go back to his hometown to get counted in a **census**.

Joseph lived in Nazareth so he had to travel back to Bethlehem. Mary went with him since they were now married. When they reached Bethlehem, it was time for Jesus to be born.

After searching for a place to stay, Joseph and Mary finally settled in a place the animals were kept because there was no room for them in any of the inns. This was exactly where God wanted Jesus to be born.

Shepherds were taking care of sheep in the fields

Emperor: The most important ruler of an empire

Census: An official count of people

near Bethlehem, just like any other night. Suddenly an angel spoke to the shepherds! The shepherds were very afraid. They had never seen an angel before. Here is what the angel said:

"Do not be afraid. I bring you good news of great joy. It is for all the people. Today in the town of David a **Savior** has been born to you. He is **Christ** the Lord."[5]

The shepherds were the first to hear the good news about Jesus.

Angel Announcing the Birth of Christ to Shepherds by Robert Leinweber

Savior: The One who saves people

Christ: The Greek word for Messiah

Now the shepherds were excited. They knew that the town of David was Bethlehem. They also knew that the Christ was the Messiah. They went to Bethlehem to look for the baby. They found Joseph, Mary, and baby Jesus lying in a manger. They visited the new family and then the shepherds left, telling everyone what the angels said.

This is a model of the temple King Herod built in Jerusalem around 9 BC. It is based on the original temple built by King Solomon nearly 1,000 years earlier.

Wikimedia Commons

Priest: Person who performs important ceremonies of faith

Joseph and Mary were Jews. Jews had many important laws to obey. And Joseph and Mary were careful to follow God's Law. Some of these were rules for parents who just had their first son.

God's Law said to take a new baby to the **priest** for a blessing. So Joseph and Mary took Jesus to the temple in Jerusalem. Jesus was 40 days old when they traveled to Jerusalem. God's Law said to make a **sacrifice** to God at the Temple. Poor people such as Mary and Joseph could sacrifice two doves, so they did.

They met an old man when they got to the temple. His name was Simeon. Simeon was very happy when he saw baby Jesus. He took Jesus in his arms. He said to God, "My eyes have seen your **salvation**."[6] Simeon was saying that he knew Jesus was the Messiah.

Another person saw Jesus at the temple. Her name was Anna. She was 84 years old! Anna stayed at the temple all day and every night. She prayed and worshipped God. She was a prophet. She had been waiting for the Messiah too. Anna was very happy when she saw baby Jesus. She told everyone about this special child.

Sacrifice: A special gift to God, such as an animal or grain

Salvation: Saving from punishment

EYEWITNESS ACCOUNT

Josephus said, "Now there was about this time Jesus, a wise man, if it be lawful to call him a man; for he was a doer of wonderful works, a teacher of such men as receive the truth with pleasure."

BIBLE HERO

Paul—Important leader of the early church, he took the Good News about Jesus all throughout the Roman Empire. Paul wrote many letters to early churches. These letters became part of the New Testament.

THE PROPHECY

Long ago, the prophet Micah said the Messiah would be born in Bethlehem. Micah 5:2 says, "The Lord says, 'Bethlehem, you might not be an important town in the nation of Judah. But out of you will come a ruler over Israel for me.'"

DID YOU KNOW?

Jesus had quite a family tree. He could trace his grandparents, great-grandparents, his great-great-great-grandparents, and the rest of his family all the way back to Adam and Eve! Here are some of the ancestors in his family tree.

Jesus
Joseph and Mary
Heli
Matthat
↑
Nathan
David
Jesse
Obed
Boaz and Ruth
Salmon and Rahab
↑
Judah
Jacob and Leah
Isaac and Rebekah
Abraham and Sarah
↑
Shem
Noah
Lamech
↑
Enosh
Seth
Adam and Eve

Chapter 3

CHILDHOOD AND YOUTH

The city of Jerusalem was a busy place. King Herod lived there in a fancy palace. Roman soldiers marched through the streets. The temple was there. There was also a busy **marketplace.** People came from miles around to buy and sell everything from food and clothes to livestock.

One day, important visitors came to Jerusalem. They had traveled very far. They came from a country in the East. These men knew how to study the movement of the stars. They were called **Wise Men**. They were looking for the King of the Jews. They had seen a special star that announced the new King's birth.

Many people think the Wise Men came from the

Marketplace: A place to buy and sell things, often outside

Wise Men: Scholars from Persia who gave gifts to Jesus

country called Persia. Today this is the countries of Iran and Iraq. Long ago, King Nebuchadnezzar of Babylonia ruled over this area. He went to war

Wikimedia Commons

The Wise Men gave Jesus special gifts of gold, incense, and myrrh.

against Israel and won. Many **captives** were taken from Israel to live in the Babylonian Empire.

Daniel was one of these captives. He was made leader of all the Wise Men. Later, this empire was conquered by the Persians. Some Bible scholars think the Wise Men who visited baby Jesus may have actually been **descendants** of Daniel and his friends.

King Herod heard about the Wise Men's journey.

Captives: People taken as prisoners

Descendants: A person's children, grandchildren, and so on

He was very upset. Herod wanted to be the one and only king! He made a secret plan to kill this new baby king and he spoke to the Wise Men, trying to get them to reveal Jesus' location.

So God gave Joseph a special dream. God warned Joseph about Herod's secret plan. Joseph was to take Mary and Jesus to Egypt. They would be safe there.

King Herod figured Jesus would be one or two years old by then. So he ordered every boy who was two years old or younger killed. Roman soldiers obeyed King Herod's command. They killed all the baby boys in Bethlehem and nearby. It was a very sad time.

Joseph and Mary stayed in Egypt until Herod died. Then God gave Joseph another dream and told him it was safe to go back to Israel. Joseph, Mary, and Jesus headed back to Israel. But Joseph heard bad news! Herod's son was now king over Judea. He was just as evil as his father.

In the dream, God told Joseph it was safe in Nazareth. A different king ruled there. So Joseph moved his family to Nazareth. They settled into a home and stayed.

What was life like for Jesus growing up in Nazareth? His family was poor like many families at the time. They most likely lived in a cave or a simple house.

Jesus had sisters and at least four brothers. His brothers' names were James, Joseph, Simon, and Judas.

Wikimedia Commons

Jesus learned to be a carpenter from his father.

His adoptive father Joseph was a **carpenter**. Jesus grew up around the smell of wood and the noise of hammers and saws. In Bible times, most sons learned the same job as their father. So Jesus learned to be a carpenter too.

Jesus attended the **synagogue** in Nazareth. Every community had a synagogue. The family went there regularly to pray. At that time, synagogues were also the local schools. That's where Jesus probably got his education. Most boys did. They learned to read the

Carpenter: Person who makes things out of wood

Synagogue: Building where Jews meet for worship

Bible. They studied the Scriptures. Girls learned at home with their mothers.

Jesus certainly did all the things that were important to the Jews and correct for boys his age. He rested on the **Sabbath**. He celebrated Jewish holidays and **feasts**. He grew up just as any other boy would during this time in Nazareth.

When Jesus was 12 years old, he went with his family to Jerusalem. It was time to celebrate Passover. They joined the big crowds who went to the capital for the feast. When the feast was over, Joseph and Mary headed home. But they soon realized they had not seen Jesus.

After three days of searching, they finally found him back at the temple in Jerusalem. Jesus was listening to the teachers and **scribes**. He asked them questions and gave them answers. People were surprised at all the things Jesus knew about God. After all, he was only 12 years old!

Sabbath: A special day of rest from Friday night to Saturday night

Feasts: Important holidays celebrated by the Jews

Scribes: Scholars who study the Scriptures and copy them by hand

Jesus at the temple when he was twelve.

DID YOU KNOW?

People today do not know for sure what kind of star the Wise Men saw. Was it a star that moved a special way in the sky? Was it a comet or planet? Or was it a special star God created just for the Wise Men to follow? We do not know. But we do know the Wise Men saw a star, and it led them to find Jesus in Bethlehem.

EYEWITNESS ACCOUNT

Josephus said, "In the fifteenth year of his reign, Herod rebuilt the temple, and encompassed a piece of land about it with a wall, which land was twice as large as that before enclosed. The expenses he laid out upon it were vastly large also, and the riches about it were unspeakable."[8]

SEVEN FEASTS

In Leviticus 23, the Bible lists seven feasts the Jews were commanded to honor.

Passover: Celebrates when God delivered Jews from the tenth plague in the book of Exodus

Unleavened Bread: Celebrates when Moses led Jews out of Egypt

Firstfruits: Celebrates the start of the spring barley harvest

Pentecost (or Weeks): Celebrates the end of harvest and when God gave the Ten Commandments to Moses

Feast of Trumpets (or Rosh Hashanah): Holy day announced with trumpet blasts

Day of Atonement (or Yom Kippur): Day when sin is paid for

Booths: Celebrates how God was with Moses and the Jews in the wilderness

Chapter 4

THE TEACHER

Jesus had a cousin named John. They were about the same age. When they were 30 years old, John was preaching God's Word. He called people to **repent**, or turn away from their sins, and turn to God. After listening to John, many people admitted the wrong things they'd done and asked God to **forgive** them. Then John **baptized** them in the Jordan River.

One day, Jesus came to be baptized by John. Jesus did not need to repent. He had never sinned or done anything wrong. In fact, John wanted to refuse to baptize Jesus.

Repent: To turn away from sins and turn toward God

Forgive: To erase the record of sins

Baptize: A symbol of being washed clean from sin through faith in God

But Jesus said to John, "Let it be this way for now. It is right for us to do this. It carries out God's holy plan."[9]

So John baptized Jesus too.

This is a popular location in the Jordan River where people go to get baptized, just like Jesus did.

Wikimedia Commons

When Jesus came up out of the water, an amazing thing happened. Heaven opened! The **Holy Spirit** came down on Jesus like a dove. God spoke and people heard his voice. God said, "This is my Son, and I love him. I am very pleased with him."[10]

Holy Spirit: The Spirit of God

After Jesus was baptized he had important work to do. But first he had to prepare. The Holy Spirit led him into the wilderness of Judea. For 40 days and 40 nights, Jesus prayed. He **fasted** and didn't eat any food. He spent time alone with God.

It was a difficult time. **Satan** came to **tempt**

This hill on the edge of the Judean wilderness is the traditional location where Jesus was tempted by Satan.

Fasted: To go without food, often during a time of prayer

Satan: The devil

Tempt: To try to get someone to do the wrong thing

Jesus with three different tests. Long ago, Satan had tempted Adam and Eve in the Garden of Eden. That's when they committed the first sin. Now Satan came to tempt Jesus. Satan tried to make Jesus sin too.

But Jesus did not sin. Instead, he turned to the Scriptures. Each time Satan tempted him, Jesus quoted a Scripture that helped him make the right choice. Finally, Satan gave up. He left Jesus alone until a later time.

Now Jesus was filled with the great power of the Holy Spirit. He returned to his hometown of Nazareth. Then he traveled to other towns and villages in Galilee. He taught in the synagogues. He preached everywhere he went. "Turn away from your sins!" Jesus said. "The **kingdom of heaven** is near."[11]

Many people started to follow Jesus. They wanted to learn more about God. These people were called disciples.

Jesus made a special team of twelve disciples. These twelve disciples were with Jesus for three years. These men were his closest friends. They traveled with him,

Kingdom of heaven: The time in history when people believe Jesus is God

learning all they could from Jesus, about God's love for the world. And they helped Jesus with his work.

So many crowds gathered around Jesus! One day, he decided to sit on a mountainside and teach. The lessons he taught that day became very famous. In the Bible, this is called the Sermon on the Mount.

The location of the Sermon on the Mount.

During the Sermon on the Mount, Jesus talked about how God blesses people. He gave many examples. These are called the Beatitudes. (Matthew 5:1–16)

He also taught people how to pray. The example he gave is called the Lord's Prayer. (Matthew 6:9–15)

Every person was important to Jesus, especially children. One day he taught about this. Jesus held children in arms. He prayed for them and blessed them.

He said, "Anyone who welcomes a little child like this in my name welcomes me."[12] Then Jesus warned people never to hurt a child or cause them to **doubt** their faith in him. He said it would be terrible if they did! Jesus said, "It would be better for him to have a large millstone hung around his neck and be drowned at the bottom of the sea."[13]

(c) Lara65/Shutterstock

A millstone was a heavy stone used to grind grain.

Often, Jesus used the Scriptures to teach people about God. He used the example of Jonah to teach people about how he would die and come alive again. He explained how

Doubt: To question if something is true

Jonah was in the belly of a fish for three days and then was spit out. Jesus said he would be in the grave for three days and then come alive again.

Jesus used the example of Noah to teach people about the future. He explained how people were busy eating and drinking. They were building and planting. They were buying and selling until the day Noah went into the **ark** and the flood came. Jesus said it would be the same one day in the future when he comes again.

Jesus taught a lawyer that the most important things in life were to love God and love other people. Jesus taught his friends Mary and Martha that life would be more meaningful if they would stop being so busy and start spending more time with God. Jesus taught a tax collector named Zacchaeus that his life could be changed after meeting Jesus.

EYEWITNESS ACCOUNT

The historian Josephus wrote that John the Baptist "was a good man, and commanded the Jews to exercise virtue, both as to righteousness towards one another, and piety towards God, and so to come to baptism."[14]

Ark: Large boat built by Noah

BIBLE HEROES

John the Baptist—To do a baptism, John stood in the river with the people. He lowered each one quickly under the water then brought them back up. This was a symbol of their faith and how God washed them clean from sin. John baptized so many people he was often called John the Baptist.

The Twelve Disciples

Peter: The leader of the disciples; a fisherman. He became a powerful preacher. Jesus said he would build his church on Peter, the Rock.

Andrew: A fisherman. Andrew was a disciple of John the Baptist before he began to follow Jesus. He brought his brother Peter to Jesus.

John: A fisherman. He possibly wrote five of the books in the Bible.

James: A fisherman. The brother of John. Jesus called these brothers the "Sons of Thunder." Later, James was the first disciple to be killed for being a Christian.

Philip: From the same town as Peter and Andrew. He brought Nathanael to meet Jesus.

Nathanael: Also called Bartholomew. A friend of Philip's from Cana in Galilee.

Thomas: After Jesus' death, believed Jesus was alive again only after he saw with his own eyes.

Matthew: A tax collector. The author of the Gospel of Matthew.

James: Perhaps also called "James the younger."

Thaddaeus: Also called Judas, the son of James.

Simon: Also called the Zealot.

Judas Iscariot: Kept charge of the disciples' money. Later, he turned Jesus over to be arrested by the Jewish leaders.

Chapter 5

STORIES AND PARABLES

One of the ways Jesus liked to teach was to tell stories. These stories are called **parables** and they taught important lessons. These parables often used everyday objects and events as examples for the people. This made the lessons easier for common people to understand and relate to.

For example, one day Jesus told a parable about a farmer planting seeds. Jesus told how some of the seeds fell on a hard path, some fell on the rocks, and some fell among thorns. None of those seeds grew.

But some of the seeds fell on good soil. These seeds grew and gave a big crop. Jesus used this parable to teach people to listen carefully to his words and

Parables: Simple stories that teach important lessons

© 1995 by Phoenix Data Systems

believe what he said, letting his message of love grow like the seeds on good soil.

Jesus told parables about farming. This is a farmer plowing his field in Israel.

Another parable was a story about three servants. A rich man was going on a trip. He gave a different amount of his money to each servant. Then he left.

Soon he came back from his trip. Two of the servants had used his money wisely. They had made more money for him. But the third servant had buried his money in a hole. He hadn't done anything with it. Jesus used this parable to teach people to share their faith. He wanted his followers to share the **Good News** and tell everyone about God.

Good News: The news that Jesus is the Messiah, the Christ

Jesus wanted to teach people about God's love. He wanted them to know God loves everyone, even people who sin. God wants everyone to turn away from their sins and turn to God.

Jesus told three parables to teach this lesson. One parable was about a lost sheep. A shepherd had 99 sheep. But one was lost. So he went looking for the lost sheep until he found it. He brought it home and **rejoiced**.

A shepherd watches over his sheep.

Rejoiced: Showed great joy

The second parable was about a lost coin. A woman had ten coins but she lost one. She cleaned her house until she found it. Then she called her neighbors to tell them the happy news.

The third parable was about a lost son. A father had two sons. One son went away, taking one half of his father's money for his own. He did bad things and wasted his money. The father thought he had died. But one day the son came back. He asked his father to forgive him. His father did and he had a big party to celebrate his son's homecoming.

Jesus told many parables. He taught the people many lessons about faith, heaven, and God.

At the time when Jesus was busiest preaching, there were three main groups of Jews. Two of these were the **Pharisees** and the **Sadducees**. Both of these groups believed different things but they were both leaders at the temple. Many of them did not like the parables Jesus told. (The **Essenes** were a third, smaller group. People from that group wrote the Dead Sea Scrolls.)

One time a group of Sadducees decided to test

Pharisees: Jewish group who followed traditions they made up

Sadducees: Jewish group who was strict about following God's Law, but did not follow the traditions of the Pharisees

Essenes: Jewish group who wrote the Dead Sea Scrolls

This scroll is part of the Dead Sea Scrolls. This is what the Bible looked like when Jesus read it.

Wikimedia Commons

Jesus. They asked Jesus who a woman would be married to in the resurrection if she had seven husbands and each of the husbands had died. The Sadducees wanted to trick Jesus, the teacher, and give him a question so hard he couldn't answer. That would surely make the people stop listening to his stories.

When Jesus heard what they said, however, he explained his thoughts to them. He also said, "You are mistaken, because you do not know the Scriptures. And you do not know the power of God."[15] The crowds were amazed at how Jesus had answered the question. Even the Sadducees couldn't trick Jesus!

Almost everyone agreed Jesus was a great teacher. But Jesus told them he was more than just a teacher. Jesus taught people that he was the Messiah, the Christ. Jesus said he was the **Son of God**.

And that's when trouble started.

Son of God: A title for Jesus meaning he is the Messiah

FAMOUS PARABLES

Jesus taught many parables. They include:

Houses on rock and on sand in Matthew 7:24–27
The mustard seed in Mark 4:30–32
The good Samaritan in Luke 10:30–37
The farmer and the seeds in Matthew 13:1–23
The lost sheep in Luke 15:1–7
The lost coin in Luke 15:8–10
The lost son in Luke 15:11–32
The rich man and Lazarus in Luke 16:19–31
Ten bridesmaids in Matthew 25:1–13
The sheep and the goats in Matthew 25:31–36

DID YOU KNOW?

• Many people in Bible times were farmers and shepherds. That's one reason why Jesus told parables about sheep and growing crops.

• Archaeologists have dug excavations of ruins from Bible times. Things they find show the Bible is a true historical document. Millar Burrows said, "Archaeological work has unquestionably strengthened confidence in the reliability of the Scriptural record. More than one archaeologist has found his respect for the Bible increased by the experience of excavation in Palestine."[16]

Chapter 6

THE SON OF GOD

You can read the Gospels today. These are the words of Jesus found in the New Testament of the Bible. You might think Jesus was only a teacher. That's because you're thinking like a person of today might think.

It's important to step back in time. Pretend to put on a pair of dusty sandals. Pretend to wear a robe. Pretend you understand how to speak **Greek** and **Aramaic**. (Greek was the language the New Testament was written. Aramaic was the language Jesus and many of the Jews spoke.)

Pretend you lived in the **culture** and the world

Greek: The language the New Testament was written in

Aramaic: The language spoken by many Jews including Jesus

Culture: The way a certain group of people dress, work, and play

that Jesus lived in. That will help you get a better understanding of what Jesus said and did.

It will also help if we look at how people reacted to Jesus. This is probably one of the best things we can do to understand who Jesus was and what he said.

For example, one day, people brought a sick man to see Jesus. The man couldn't walk, so they carried him on a mat. Jesus looked at the man. He said, "Son, your sins are forgiven."[17]

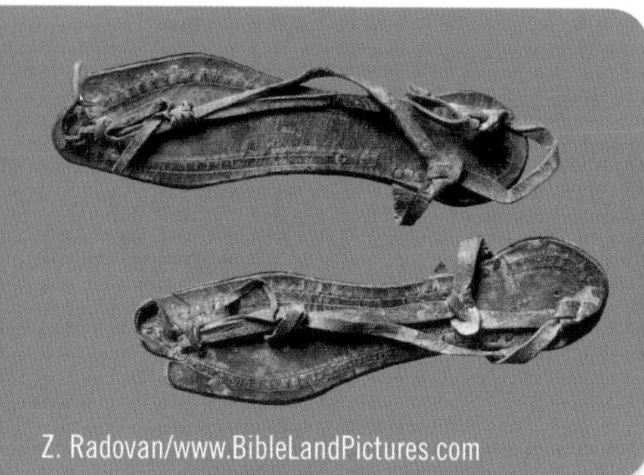

Z. Radovan/www.BibleLandPictures.com

These leather sandals are from the first century, around the time when Jesus lived.

How did people react? There were teachers of the law sitting there. They were upset. They were thinking, "He's saying a very evil thing! Only God can forgive sins!"[18] They knew Jesus said he was God.

Another time, Jesus was at the temple area. He was talking with the Jews about Abraham. Jesus told them Abraham was filled with joy about him and his work.

How did the people react? "You are not even 50

years old," the Jews said to Jesus. "And you have seen Abraham?"[19]

They were upset because Jesus made it sound like he talked with Abraham. Abraham had lived over 2,000 years before Jesus was born.

But what Jesus said next made the people even angrier.

Wikimedia Commons

One day Peter, James, and John saw Jesus change when he was praying. His clothes became bright white. His face shone as the sun. Then he talked with Moses and Elijah, two Old Testament prophets. This is called the Transfiguration.

"What I'm about to tell you is true," Jesus answered. "Before Abraham was born, **I am**!"[20]

I am: A special name for God meaning he is alive forever

This time, the people picked up stones to throw at him. Stones were what people used in Bible times to punish and kill people. And they were so angry they wanted to kill Jesus!

Why? Because long ago Moses talked with God about leading the Israelites out of Egypt. God spoke to Moses through a burning bush. When Moses asked God what his name was, God said, "I am."

Jesus had just told the Jews that he had talked with someone who lived over 2,000 years ago. He had just told them his name was "I am." In other words, Jesus had just told them he was God. And that made them **furious** enough to want to kill him.

Even when his own family heard the things Jesus was saying and doing, they questioned his words and actions. Once they went to the house where he was teaching. They told people, "He is out of his mind."[21]

Not everyone was upset when Jesus said he was God. One day Jesus met a woman at Jacob's Well in the region of Samaria. Jesus told her who he was. How did this woman react? She was so excited she went back home and told all her friends. Many people from her town

Furious: Very angry

Jacob's Well in Samaria.
LOC, LC-DIG-matpc–00040

came to meet Jesus. After they spent time with him, how did they react? They said, "We know that this man really is the Savior of the world."[22]

One day Jesus asked Peter, "Who do you say I am?"[23]

Peter answered, "You are the Christ.[24] You are the Son of the living God."

This time it was Jesus' turn to react. What did he do? Jesus said, "**Blessed** are you!"[25] Then Jesus told Peter that he would be the rock on which Jesus would build his church. Jesus saw that Peter finally understood what he had been saying all along.

Jesus was teaching people that he was the Christ. Jesus said he was the Messiah, the one the Jews had been waiting for.

Blessed: Someone who has been given good gifts from God

But he didn't just *say* that he was God. He showed them too.

THE NAME OF GOD

When Moses asked God to say his name, God said, "I AM." The Gospel of John quotes seven times that Jesus said, "I AM." Each time Jesus said this he was telling people he was God.

DID YOU KNOW?

Samaria had been conquered by different rulers over the years so the faith of the Samaritans was different than the Jews. They did not follow the same laws or believe the same things. Most Samaritans and Jews would not talk with each other for this reason.

BIBLE HERO

The Woman at the Well—The woman Jesus spoke with was an ordinary woman, but she did an extraordinary thing. She told others about Jesus. Because of her witness, many people believed Jesus was the Messiah, the Christ.

DID YOU KNOW?

In Bible times, women were second-class citizens. They did not have many rights. They were not considered as important as men. Jesus was different. He treated women with kindness and respect. His example shows each person is valuable to God.

Chapter 7

MIRACLES

The Jews were waiting and waiting for the Messiah, the Christ. They expected Christ to come at any time. During Jesus' time, many Jews thought Christ would deliver them from the Romans. People even asked John the Baptist if he was the Christ. He said no but he said that Christ was coming soon.

How would they recognize Christ? Many prophets had said there would be different **signs** to watch for. The prophet Isaiah, for example, said the Messiah would do many **miracles**. This would be one sign the people could see.

The Gospels record many miracles Jesus did. The books of Matthew and John are both eyewitness

Signs: Clues that help show what is true

Miracles: Amazing events that only God can do

Wikimedia Commons

Jesus told the blind man to wash in the Pool of Siloam. Then he could see. It was a miracle.

accounts of many of those miracles. As two of the twelve disciples, Matthew and John were with Jesus for three years. They wrote down the things they actually saw.

One Sabbath day for example, Jesus healed a blind man. The book of John tells what happened next.

When the man's neighbors found out his wonderful news, they wanted to know how the man could now see. The man told them, "The man they call Jesus made some mud and put it on my eyes. He told me to go to Siloam and wash. So I went and washed."

"Where is this man?" they asked him.

"I don't know," he said.[26]

Some people **insisted** that the man couldn't be

Insisted: Strongly said

the same one who was born blind. Others said it was. Everyone was confused. Nothing like this had ever happened before.

The Pharisees heard about this. They talked with the man too.

The Pharisees were trying to decide if Jesus really was the Messiah. Some of them said he couldn't be. They did not think someone from God would do a miracle on the Sabbath. Other Pharisees argued that only someone from God could make a blind man see no matter what day it was.

The Jewish leaders couldn't agree so they called in the cured man's parents. They questioned them. His parents said this was definitely their son. He was born blind and now he could see.

The Jewish leaders called the man to the synagogue again. They said there was no way to know if Jesus really was from God. The man disagreed. He said, "Nobody has ever heard of anyone opening the eyes of a person born blind. If this man had not come from God, he could do nothing."[27]

They were upset with his words. They threw the man out of the synagogue.

Later Jesus found the man he had cured. Jesus told him who he was and asked if he believed. The man told Jesus, "Lord, I believe."[28] He was saying he believed Jesus was the Messiah, the Christ.

And many others believed Jesus was the Messiah too. They believed this because of the miracles Jesus did.

Matthew gave an eyewitness account of another miracle. Matthew wrote, "Jesus went through all the towns and villages. He taught in their synagogues.

Jesus did many of his miracles near the Sea of Galilee.

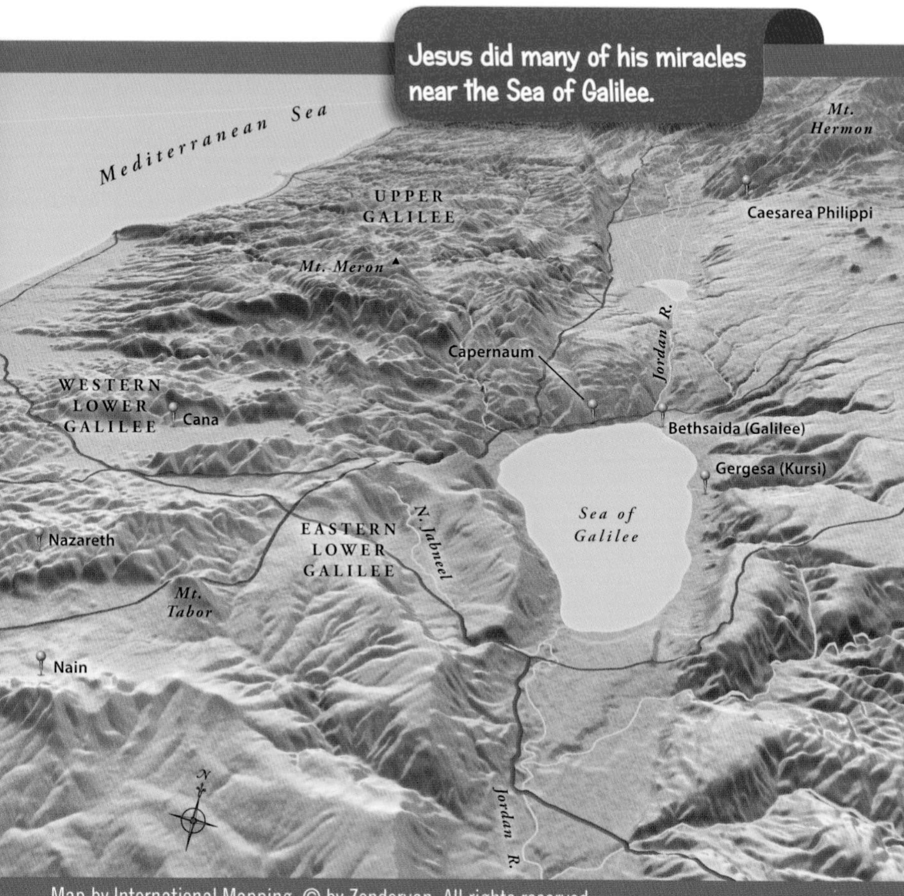

He preached the good news of the kingdom. And he healed every illness and sickness."[29]

One day, Jesus did one of the most amazing miracles of all. He brought a dead man back to life. Many people were filled with joy. But the Pharisees and **chief priests** were very upset about this. They immediately called a special meeting of the **Sanhedrin**.

"What can we do?" they asked at the meeting. "This man is doing many miraculous signs. If we let him keep on doing this, everyone will believe in him. Then the Romans will come. They will take away our temple and our nation."[30]

The Jewish leaders did not want this to happen. Many Bible scholars agree that from that day on, they made plans to kill Jesus.

THE MESSIAH

The prophet Isaiah said the Messiah would be recognized by the miracles he does. Isaiah said, "Then the eyes of those who are blind will be opened. The ears of those who can't hear will be unplugged. Those who can't walk will leap like a deer. And those who can't speak will shout with joy."
Isaiah 35:5–6, NIrV

Chief priests: A group of official Jewish leaders

Sanhedrin: The highest group of Jewish leaders who met in Jerusalem and made important decisions

EYEWITNESS ACCOUNT

John was an eyewitness to many miracles Jesus did. He documents seven key miracles in the Gospel of John.

1. Jesus turns water into wine. (John 2:1–11)
2. Jesus heals an official's son from a high fever. (John 4:43–54)
3. Jesus heals a man who cannot walk. (John 5:1–15)
4. Jesus feeds 5,000 people with five loaves of bread and two fish. (John 6:1–14)
5. Jesus walks on water. (John 6:16–21)
6. Jesus heals a blind man. (John 9:1–41)
7. Jesus raises a dead man back to life. (John 11:1–45)

BIBLE HERO

Isaiah—A prophet who wrote about the coming of the Messiah. The book of Isaiah is one of the most read books in the Old Testament.

DEATH TO LIFE

The Gospels document three times Jesus brought people back to life.

- A ruler's daughter in Matthew 9:18–25.
- A widow's son in Luke 7:11–15.
- Lazarus, Jesus' friend in John 11:1–44.

DID YOU KNOW?

Leprosy is a terrible skin disease. One time, Jesus healed ten men who had leprosy. Only one thanked Jesus. He was from Samaria.

Chapter 8

PREPARING FOR PASSOVER

All throughout the region, the Jews were preparing for Passover. As always, every obedient Jew was headed to Jerusalem to celebrate the feast. Passover, as well as Pentecost and Booths, were three of the most important feasts to Jews. And all Jews were expected to travel to Jerusalem every year to celebrate each of these feasts if they could.

Jesus and his disciples walked to Jerusalem. On the way, Jesus had a special message to tell the twelve disciples. He told them, "We are going up to Jerusalem. The **Son of Man** will be handed over to the chief priests and the teachers of the law."

Jesus also said, "They will sentence him to death.

Son of Man: A title Jesus used to show that even though he was God, he had come to earth as a man

Jerusalem at the time of Jesus.

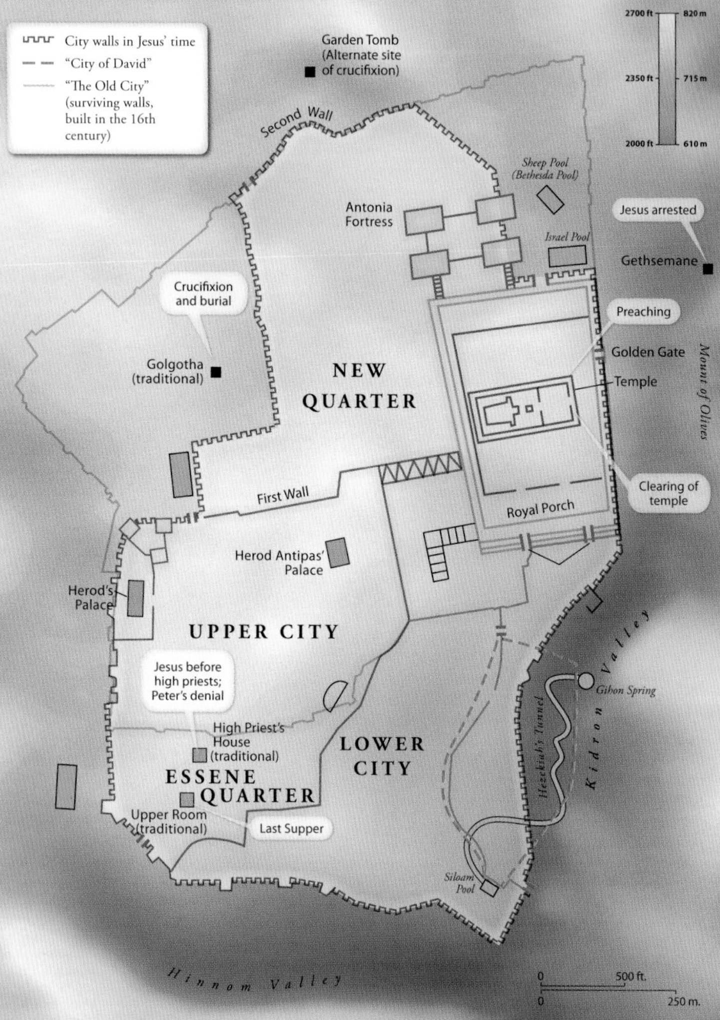

Then they will turn him over to people who are not Jews. The people will make fun of him and whip him. They will nail him to a **cross**. On the third day, he will rise from the dead!"[31]

The disciples felt afraid. They didn't know what to think. What was Jesus talking about?

Many scholars agree that Jesus knew it was dangerous to go to Jerusalem. Jewish leaders were there. They wanted to have Jesus killed and were not secretive about it. Roman officials were there. They were eager to kill anyone they thought did not worship Caesar or their gods.

Jesus knew what was ahead of him in Jerusalem. He knew an important time had come in God's plan.

At this time, Jesus stopped in the village of Bethany. He had dinner with his friends Lazarus, Martha, and Mary. Lazarus was at the table with Jesus. The disciples were there too. Martha was serving the meal.

Mary brought in a jar of expensive perfume. She **anointed** Jesus with the perfume. She poured it over his head and his feet. Then she dried his feet with her hair.

Cross: Two pieces of wood put together in the shape of a T that Romans used to kill criminals by hanging them on it

Anointed: To put oil or perfume on someone in a special way

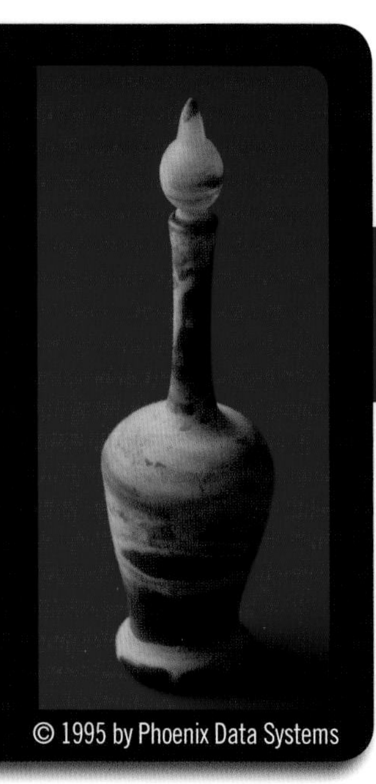

Glass perfume bottles from the time of Jesus.

Some of the people were upset. They said Mary should have sold the perfume. Then she could give the money to the poor.

But Jesus asked, "Why are you bothering this woman? She has done a beautiful thing for me." Then he said, "She poured the perfume on my body to prepare me to be buried."[32]

Once again, Jesus let everyone know that he was going to die very soon.

Jesus had gone to Jerusalem many times before. This time was different, however. This time he rode into Jerusalem on a donkey's **colt**. Crowds of people were everywhere. Some threw their robes down on the street in front of Jesus. Others threw down palm branches. Jesus rode over these as he entered Jerusalem.

Many people in the crowds believed Jesus was the

Colt: Young donkey or horse

Messiah. They shouted, "**Hosanna**! Blessed is the one who comes in the name of the Lord! Blessed is the King of Israel!"[33]

This made the Jewish leaders angrier than ever. They still wanted to stop Jesus and his preaching. They kept looking for a reason to kill Jesus. And then they found it.

Judas Iscariot was one of Jesus' twelve disciples. He was in charge of their money. He used to take some of the money for himself.

Judas made a deal with the Jewish leaders. He would watch for a good time, then he would lead them to Jesus. The chief priests paid Judas 30 pieces of silver to do this.

It was a busy week for Jesus in Jerusalem. He visited the temple. It was crowded with visitors who had come to celebrate the Passover. Men had tables set up in the temple area. They were buying and selling things. They were making a huge **profit**.

Some of the men were money changers. At these tables, people exchanged Roman coins for special coins used at the temple. At other tables, people could buy doves and other animals to sacrifice during Passover.

Hosanna: Word meaning "save"

Profit: A lot of money a seller can keep

The temple in Jesus' day.

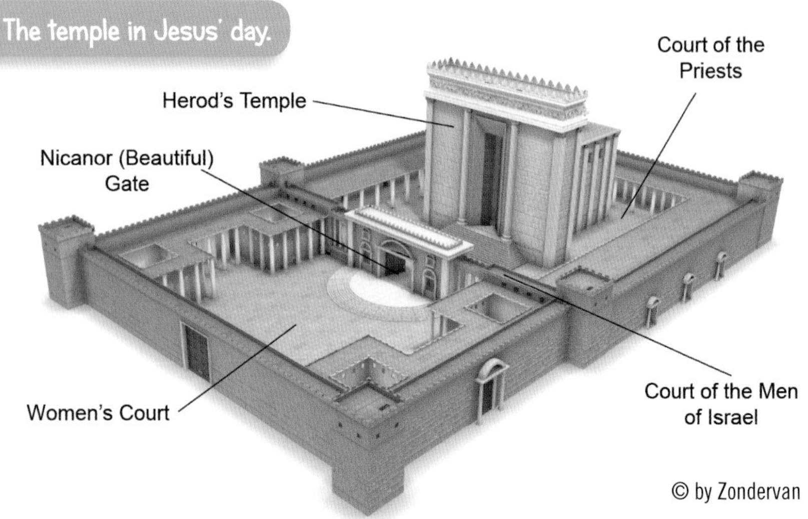

Jesus was very upset this was happening in his Father's house. He turned over these tables. He made the **dishonest** men leave. He said to them, "It is written that the Lord said, 'My house will be called a house where people can pray.' But you are making it a 'den for robbers.' "[34]

The chief priests and lawyers did not like what Jesus had done. They wanted to know who gave him the right to throw the men out of the temple.

This was the day of preparation for the Passover

Dishonest: People who cheat or lie

feast. Jesus celebrated a special Passover with his twelve disciples. They ate a feast together. It was a very special time for them.

This bread and this cup may be like the ones Jesus shared with his disciples at the Last Supper.

© IngridHS/Shutterstock

During this time together, Jesus washed the disciples' feet. This was to show them they must be willing to serve others. He shared bread and the cup of wine with them—their last meal together. He prayed. Each of the things Jesus did held special meaning.

After supper, Jesus took some of his disciples out of the city. They walked to a nearby garden. The **Garden of Gethsemane** was on a hill called the **Mount** of Olives. The disciples slept in the garden. Thousands of people were camping all over the fields and hills around Jerusalem. But Jesus didn't sleep. He stayed up all night to pray.

Garden of Gethsemane: A garden near Jerusalem

Mount: A mountain or hill

In the gospel of Matthew, it says as he prayed, Jesus talked to God. He said, "My Father, if it is possible, take this cup of suffering away from me."[35]

It was as if Jesus was asking God if there was any other way to take care of the sin problem. This was the sin problem that began in another garden over 2,500 years before when Adam and Eve were in the Garden of Eden and when sin entered the world.

Jesus spent his last night praying in the Garden of Gethsemane.

But God was silent. There was no other way to take care of the sin problem. The cross was the only answer. It was part of God's plan.

Finally, Jesus finished praying. He told God, "Let what you want be done, not what I want."[36] He chose to be **obedient** to God's plan.

He went and woke up his disciples. Then Jesus said, "The hour has come. Look! The Son of Man is about to be handed over to sinners. Get up! Let us go! Here comes the one who is handing me over to them!"[37]

JERUSALEM'S KING

Long ago, the prophet Zechariah talked about the Messiah. He said the Messiah would come into Jerusalem riding on a donkey. He said,

> "City of Zion, be full of joy!
> People of Jerusalem, shout!
> See, your king comes to you.
> He always does what is right.
> He has the power to save.
> He is gentle and riding on a donkey.
> He is sitting on a donkey's colt."

Zechariah 9:9[38]

Obedient: To do what you're told

DID YOU KNOW?

• A lamb was offered as a special sacrifice at Passover. It had to be perfect and could not be sick or hurt. The first Passover was in Egypt. The blood of the Passover lamb protected the Israelite families from the death of the firstborn son. In Jesus' day, the Passover was a time to remember when God delivered Moses and the Jews from bondage. It was a time to look for the Messiah to come deliver them again.

• Sir Robert Anderson was a police detective for England's Scotland Yard. He knew the book of Daniel said the exact date the Messiah would enter Jerusalem but it was tricky to figure out.

One reason was because different nations used different calendars. Daniel was from the nation of Israel but he lived in Babylon. Different nations ruled over him at different times.

So Sir Anderson did some investigating. Then he did some math. He figured out that Daniel 9 said the Messiah would enter Jerusalem on the exact day Jesus rode the donkey into Jerusalem!

THE MESSIAH ENTERS JERUSALEM

Jesus expected the Jews to know the exact day the Messiah would enter Jerusalem. He held them responsible for this. Luke 19:41–44 says that Jesus approached Jerusalem. "When he saw the city, he began to sob. He said, 'I wish you had known today what would bring your peace! But now it is hidden from your eyes. The days will come when your enemies will arrive. They will build a wall of dirt up against your city. They will surround you and close you in on every side. You didn't recognize the time when God came to you.'"

Chapter 9

A SAD DAY

A crowd of chief priests and **elders** came to the garden where Jesus had been praying. They were armed with clubs and swords. Judas was leading them. He greeted Jesus with a kiss of friendship. This was the signal to arrest Jesus.

Jesus let the soldiers arrest him. He did not fight back. He was not afraid. He said, "All this has happened so that the words of the prophets would come true."[39]

The disciples were afraid though. Some of them ran away. Others followed at a distance.

First, the soldiers took Jesus to the house of Annas. Annas had once been **high priest**. They tried to find a reason to have Jesus killed. Annas sent Jesus to his

Elders: Leaders of the Jews

High priest: The leader of all the priests

son-in-law Caiaphas. Caiaphas was the high priest that year. John, one of twelve disciples, knew the high priest so he was allowed to follow Jesus inside.

Wikimedia Commons

This box holds the bones of Caiaphas, the high priest.

John was an eyewitness to the events that happened to Jesus that day. In the Gospel of John, he recorded the details as he saw them. Scholars consider this gospel account as a very **reliable** source of information.

The Sanhedrin gathered at the high priest's house. They tried to find a reason to have Jesus killed too. They spent most of the time arguing. Different people told lies about Jesus. Nobody could agree what to do.

Finally, Caiaphas asked Jesus, "Are you the Christ? Are you the Son of the Blessed One?"

"I am," said Jesus.[40]

Many scholars agree that Jesus had just announced

Reliable: Trusted as true

he was the Messiah! People were not **misinterpreting** Jesus' teachings. Jesus clearly said he was God.

Pilate presents Jesus to the crowds.

Wikimedia Commons

Misinterpreting: Thinking something is different than what was said

How did the people react? At this answer, the high priest tore his robes. The leaders said Jesus should be killed for this crime.

So next they sent Jesus to the Romans. The Romans were the only ones who actually had the power to sentence anyone to death. Pilate was the Roman governor of Judea. He found nothing wrong with Jesus. Jesus was innocent. So Pilate sent him to King Herod and King Herod sent Jesus back to Pilate.

By now, the chief priests and leaders were starting a **riot**. The crowd was getting out of control. Now it seemed Jesus might be a political **threat** to Rome. So Pilate finally agreed to do what the crowd wanted. He sent Jesus to the cross, which was one way criminals were put to death.

Jesus was ordered to carry his own cross through the streets but he was too weak. He had been beaten and whipped while they were questioning him. A crown of thorns had been put on his head. He had lost a lot of blood.

Roman soldiers pulled a man named Simon from the crowd. Simon carried the cross for Jesus for a while.

Riot: When a large group of people start acting angry and sometimes hurt others

Threat: Something that might hurt others

They headed outside the city to a place called the Skull. Here they nailed Jesus to the cross. Pilate ordered a sign hung at the top of the cross. It said, "This is Jesus the King of the Jews."[41]

Jesus died on a cross between two criminals.

© Providence Collection/www.GoodSalt.com

While Jesus hung on the cross, most Jews were at the temple. They were sacrificing lambs there for their sins. It was just before the Passover feast. The followers of Jesus stood near the cross and watched. Mary, his mother, and other women were there too.

John was also at Calvary. Once again, John was an eyewitness. He wrote about the details of the death of Jesus as he saw them.

As Jesus died, strange things happened. The sun stopped shining even though it was the middle of the day. It got very, very dark.

Jesus called out, "Father, into your hands I **commit** my very life."[42] He took one last breath. Then he died.

The large curtain in the temple was suddenly torn. It was ripped from top to bottom—and not by human hands.

When Jesus died, the curtain in the temple was ripped from top to bottom. This showed the way to God was now open through Jesus.

The earth shook from a big earthquake. Rocks split open.

Tombs opened in the graveyards. Dead people came back to life.

The Roman soldiers saw these things happen. They were afraid!

Even the **centurion**, a commander in the Roman army spoke up. He said, "This man was surely the Son of God!"[43]

Commit: To give

Tombs: Caves or boxes that hold the bodies of dead people

Centurion: A leader over 100 soldiers in the Roman army

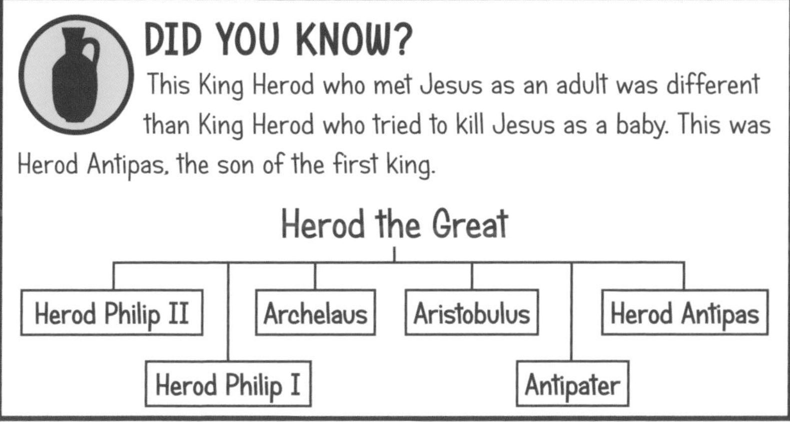

KING DAVID'S PSALM

Jesus quoted Psalm 22:1 while he was on the cross. He said, "My God, My God, why have you deserted me?" Psalm 22 describes many details about the death of Jesus. Yet it was written about 1,000 years earlier, by King David!

EYEWITNESS ACCOUNT

In the Gospel of John, John writes his eyewitness account of Jesus' death on the cross. John 19:35 says, "The man who saw it has given witness. And his witness is true. He knows that he tells the truth. He gives witness so that you also can believe."

EYEWITNESS ACCOUNT

Tacitus lived less than 100 years after Jesus. He wrote about how Christians were being killed at that time. He also mentioned the death of Jesus Christ. He said, "Christus, from whom the name had its origin, suffered the extreme penalty during the reign of Tiberius at the hands of one of our procurators, Pontius Pilatus."[44]

Chapter 10

UNEXPECTED NEWS

After Jesus died, a follower of Jesus went to see Pilate. His name was Joseph. He was very rich. He asked Pilate if he could have the body of Jesus for burial. Pilate gave him **permission**. Joseph took the body of Jesus,

This 2,000 year old stone has Pontius Pilate's name on it. It says Pilate was the governor of Judea.

G.dallorto/Wikimedia Commons

wrapped it in clean strips of cloth, and put it in his own

Permission: To let someone do something

tomb. Then he had a very large stone rolled across the entrance.

Pilate had other visitors. The chief priests went to Pilate. They said, "We remember something that Jesus said while he was still alive. He claimed, 'After three days I will rise again.' So give the order to make the tomb **secure** until the third day. If you don't, his disciples might come and steal the body. Then they will tell the people that Jesus has been raised from the dead. This last lie will be worse than the first."

G.dallorto/Wikimedia Commons

This carving shows Roman soldiers.

"Take some guards with you," Pilate answered. "Make the tomb as secure as you can."[45]

So they did. They put a **seal** on the large stone. They got Roman soldiers to stand guard.

Secure: Make safe from attack or robbers

Seal: A special kind of lock

The chief priests were finally satisfied. They had gotten rid of Jesus.

Or had they?

At **dawn** on Sunday morning, several women walked to the tomb of Jesus. They had prepared special spices. They planned to put the spices on the dead body of Jesus. This was a common **custom** at that time.

A large stone was put over the door of the tomb. This kept away thieves and wild animals.

© William D. Mounce

Dawn: The first sunlight in the morning

Custom: Common action of a group who live in the same area

But the women were worried. How would they roll away the big stone from the entrance of the tomb? It probably weighed two tons! It was too big for them to move.

Suddenly the ground shook. There was a huge earthquake. An angel appeared. He glowed like lightning. The angel rolled back the stone and sat on it.

Roman soldiers were guarding the tomb. They saw the angel. They were terrified and they fainted from fear and fell on the ground.

The angel spoke to the women. He told them Jesus was alive again. He had risen from the dead! The angel then told the women to tell this good news to the disciples. The women were filled with both fear and joy. They ran quickly to tell the others.

Some of the disciples did not believe them. John and Peter raced back to the **graveyard**. When they saw the empty tomb, they believed the women's words.

By now, the Roman guards were awake. They knew they were in serious trouble. They could be killed for letting all this happen! So the guards hurried to the chief priests. They told them everything that had happened.

Graveyard: Place where dead people are buried

The chief priests **panicked**. They held an emergency meeting. Then they came up with a plan. They paid the Roman soldiers a **bribe** and told them to tell everyone the disciples had stolen the body of Jesus.

The soldiers took the money. They spread the lie. Many believed them.

Soon, other news was heard. Some people said they had seen Jesus. They said Jesus was alive again!

All Jerusalem was stirred up. What was going on?

EYEWITNESS ACCOUNT

Josephus said, "The Jews used to take so much care of the burial of men, that they took down those that were condemned and crucified, and buried them before the going down of the sun."[46]

DID YOU KNOW?

In Bible times, the body of a dead person was washed. Then it was rubbed with perfumed oils, wrapped in strips of white cloths, and put in a tomb.

Panicked: So afraid someone doesn't know what to do

Bribe: Money paid to get someone to do something wrong

DID YOU KNOW?

Poor people were buried in public graveyards. Other people had tombs in caves or graves on their own land. Rich people built tombs out of rock. There were shelves to place dead bodies on. After a dead body rotted away, the bones were put in a stone box. Then another dead body could be put on the shelf.

ANGELS

The Bible says that angels are mighty warriors. They have important jobs to do. Psalms 103:20–21 says, "Praise the Lord, you angels of his. Praise him, you mighty ones who carry out his orders and obey his word. Praise the Lord, all you angels in heaven. Praise him, all you who serve him and do what he wants."

Chapter 11

A NEW PURPOSE

Three days after Jesus had been crucified, some of the women stood near his tomb. Mary Magdalene was one of them. She was crying. She thought someone had stolen the body of Jesus.

Suddenly Jesus appeared to her. He said, "Go to those who believe in me. Tell them 'I am returning to my Father and your Father, to my God and your God.' "[47]

On Sunday, Jesus came alive again. The tomb was empty.

That same day, two men were walking on a road. They

were going from Jerusalem to the village of Emmaus. Jesus came up and walked with them. At first they did not **recognize** Jesus. They told him how Jesus had been killed on the cross. So Jesus explained to them all the Scriptures about the Messiah from the Old Testament.

At the end of their journey they were eating together and Jesus shared bread with them. Finally they realized they were talking with Jesus! The two men hurried back to Jerusalem to tell the disciples. They had seen Jesus!

The disciples were meeting in an upstairs room of a home. Only ten of the disciples were there. Thomas was not, nor was Judas. Judas had felt so terrible about his part in what had happened that he had killed himself.

The disciples felt afraid. They did not want to get **arrested** and killed like Jesus. So they locked the door of the room where they were staying.

But Jesus still came in and stood with them. This surprised them! How had he gotten inside? The door was locked. They thought they were seeing a ghost.

So Jesus showed them his hands and feet. They

Recognize: Know who someone is

Arrested: Caught by the police or soldiers

could see the **scars** where the soldiers nailed him to the cross. Jesus showed them his side. They could see the scar where a soldier hurt him with a spear. Finally, the disciples believed Jesus was God. They were filled with joy.

Then Jesus did something very special. He breathed on them. He said, "Receive the Holy Spirit."[48] Jesus gave them the Holy Spirit to live inside them after they believed.

The risen Jesus had breakfast with his disciples at the Sea of Galilee.

© Providence Collection/www.GoodSalt.com

When Thomas heard what happened, he still did not believe Jesus had risen from the dead. He said he wouldn't believe unless he saw Jesus and touched Jesus' scars himself.

Scars: Marks left on the skin after being hurt

After that, Jesus appeared to his followers at different times. He appeared to Thomas, and Thomas believed. He appeared to the disciples by the Sea of Galilee and cooked breakfast for them. He appeared to a **crowd** of over 500 of his followers. He even appeared to his own brother, James.

Jesus appeared to his followers for 40 days. During that time they ate together. They talked with him and asked him questions. Jesus explained many things to the disciples about God and his kingdom.

One question they asked Jesus was, "Are you going to give the kingdom back to Israel now?"[49] They still thought the Messiah would deliver Israel from Roman rule.

Jesus told them not to worry about that. Instead, he **instructed** them to wait together in Jerusalem. He said he would give them power from the Holy Spirit. Then they would go all over the world to tell people about Jesus, the Christ.

After teaching his followers these things, Jesus took them out toward the village of Bethany. He gave them one final **blessing**.

Crowd: Large group of people

Instructed: Told what to do

Blessing: God giving good gifts

The Mount of Olives is where the risen Jesus was taken up to heaven.

Then Jesus ascended into the air. His followers watched this amazing thing happen. Up and up he rose until a cloud hid him.

They **stared** up at the sky. Suddenly, two angels stood next to them. They said, “Why do you stand

Stared: Looked at something a long time

here looking at the sky? Jesus has been taken away from you into heaven. But he will come back in the same way you saw him go."

With that, the disciples returned to Jerusalem. They waited in the upstairs room. Eleven disciples were there with Jesus' mother Mary. So were his brothers and some other women too. They met together and prayed.

The disciples picked a new man to take the place of Judas. They chose Matthias, a follower of Jesus since the days of John the Baptist.

The day of Pentecost arrived. This was an important feast. If they could, every Jew was supposed to travel to Jerusalem to celebrate. Jerusalem was crowded with Jews from every country in the Roman Empire.

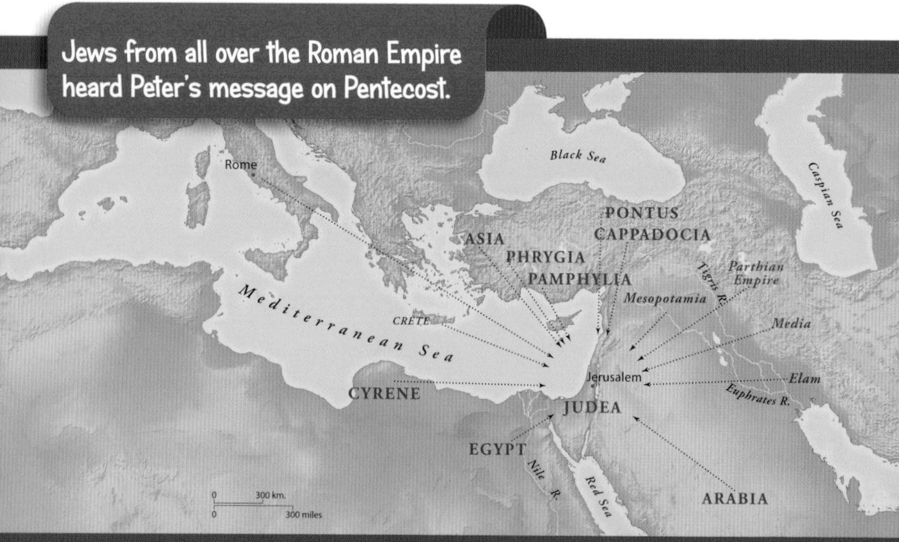

Jews from all over the Roman Empire heard Peter's message on Pentecost.

Pentecost

Planet Art

Jesus' followers were meeting again. Suddenly, a loud sound filled the whole house. It sounded like the wind. Then it looked like **flames** of fire were burning on top of each person's head. Everyone was filled with the **presence** of the Holy Spirit. Each one began talking in languages they had never learned.

The sound was so loud a crowd rushed to the house. Everyone was surprised to hear about their salvation with Jesus in their own language.

What was going on?

Peter stood up and spoke to the crowd. He explained that Jesus had just sent the Holy Spirit. He told them how Jesus had died on the cross. His blood was the sacrifice that paid the price for their sins.

Peter told them, "God has raised this same Jesus back to life. We are all **witnesses** of this."

Three thousand people in the crowd heard these words. Now they believed in Jesus too and were all baptized. The new church had begun to grow.

Flames: The part of fire that burns very bright

Presence: Someone who is there even if you can't see him

Witnesses: People who see something with their own eyes

BIBLE HERO

Mary Magdalene—The first person to see Jesus after he rose from the dead.

DID YOU KNOW?

The Feast of Pentecost celebrated the end of the harvest. It was a time to remember when God gave Moses the Ten Commandments. This was also the day Jesus sent the power of the Holy Spirit to the early church.

PROPHECIES FOR THE MESSIAH

The Old Testament lists many things about the Messiah. It was written hundreds and thousands of years before Jesus was born. Jesus fulfilled all of these things.

The Bible says the Messiah would:

- Be a descendant of David (2 Samuel 7:12)
- Be born of a virgin (Isaiah 7:14)
- Be born in Bethlehem (Micah 5:2)
- Teach with parables (Psalm 78:2)
- Ride on a donkey into Jerusalem as king (Zechariah 9:9)
- Be betrayed for 30 pieces of silver (Zechariah 11:12)
- Have nails in his hands (Psalm 22:14–17)
- Sentenced to die (Isaiah 53:7–9)
- Come to life again (Psalm 16:10)

DID YOU KNOW?

Different people have done the math. They've figured out how likely it would be for one person to fulfill every single prophecy about the Messiah. The number has more zeros than one in a billion! Many scholars agree this proves that Jesus is actually who he said he was ... the Messiah, the Christ.

Chapter 12

THE FUTURE

The Jewish leaders were upset about what was happening. They arrested Peter and John. They questioned them, and what they found amazed them.

They had seen these men earlier. Peter and John were not **educated**. They were common fishermen. During the arrest of Jesus, they had been afraid. Yet now Peter and John were so **bold**! And they spoke so well! The Jewish leaders realized they'd been with Jesus and Jesus had changed them. They **released** Peter and John and warned them never to say another word about Jesus.

But the believers had to share what they knew. They wanted to tell others what they'd seen. They

Educated: Someone who had been taught in a school

Bold: Not scared

Released: Let go

wanted to tell others about Jesus and they wanted others to experience salvation too.

Many historians and scholars agree—these people actually saw Jesus alive again. Otherwise they would not have changed like they did.

Years went by. The church grew and grew. The believers spread the news about Jesus. They went all over the Roman Empire. People who believed became known as Christians. This meant Christ followers. The Christians faced **persecution**. Many were killed. The

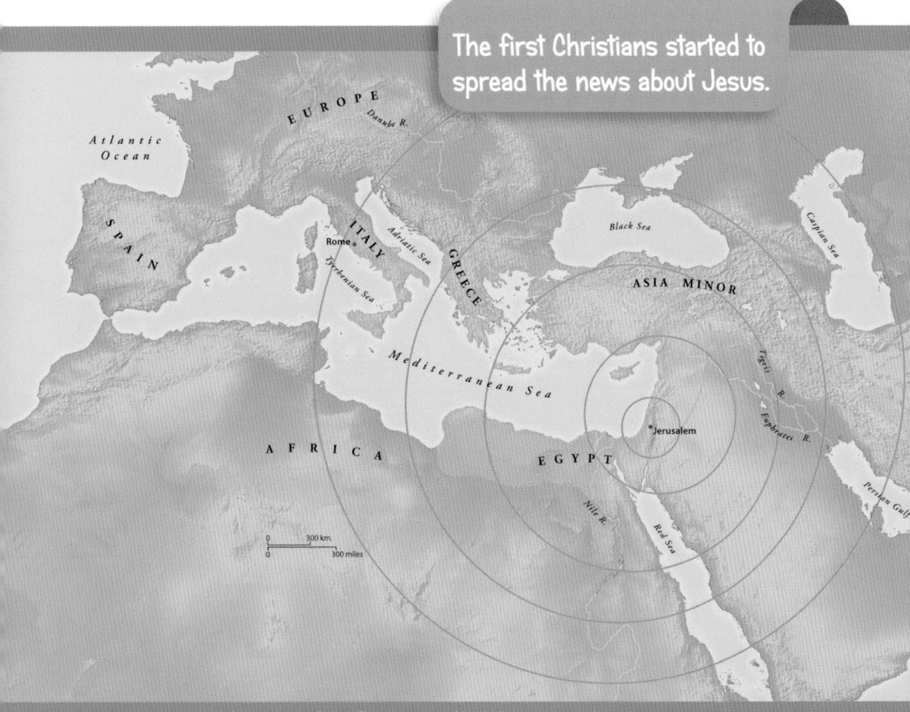

The first Christians started to spread the news about Jesus.

Roman Empire did not allow people to follow any leader except Caesar. They made everyone worship their own gods and they punished Christians.

When he was very old, John was punished for believing. He was forced to live alone on an island called Patmos. While there, he received a message from Jesus.

The first part of the message was for seven of the churches. It was a warning to follow the teachings of Jesus. It was an **encouragement** to stay strong in their faith.

John heard a special message from Jesus on the island of Patmos. This became Revelation, the last book of the Bible.

The last part of the message was about the future. Jesus told John what was going to happen in the world. It was part of God's plan. This plan explained how the Messiah would take care of the sin problem forever. Jesus

Persecution: Hurting or killing people because of their beliefs

Encouragement: Something that gives hope and courage

said that a time of **judgment** was coming. God gave Jesus the authority to judge. This was because of the sacrifice Jesus made—dying on the cross for people's sins.

John saw a Book of Judgment in heaven. It was closed with seven seals. Jesus was the only one worthy to open those seals. The seven seals would be opened. Then seven angels would blow their trumpets. This would warn people that Satan would try to **defeat** God's followers.

Then the seven angels would empty seven bowls. This would show God's power against Satan. Many people would decide to follow Satan. But then the kingdoms of earth will be destroyed.

At that time, Jesus will return to earth. He will ride on a white horse. He will lead the armies of heaven. Jesus will lock up Satan and his helpers. He will **establish** his throne in Jerusalem. Jesus will rule as king over the earth. This will be for 1,000 years.

After that, Satan will be let go. Satan will try to defeat God's people again. But Jesus will defeat Satan forever.

A new heaven and a new earth will be established. Jesus will rule forever in the new city of Jerusalem. There

Judgment: To make a decision, often between good and evil

Defeat: To beat someone, usually in battle

Establish: Make

will never again be any evil, **sorrow**, or tears. People will live in the loving presence of God forever. It was a promise Jesus gave to John.

Jesus said he will come again. He will ride on a white horse and lead the armies of heaven.

That was the end of the message.

John wrote down the message from Jesus. It became the book of Revelation—the last book in the Bible.

This message gave hope to Christians as never before. They knew Jesus was coming back. They knew God's love would **triumph** over evil. They knew what was going to happen in the future. They knew God would keep his promise, just as he'd already done. They knew it was part of God's plan. The plan for Jesus, the Messiah to be here for all.

Sorrow: Feeling sad

Triumph: Win

DID YOU KNOW?

Justin Martyr, Eusebius, Tertullian, and Polycarp are some of the early church fathers. They quoted the New Testament more than 86,000 times in their writings. You can still read their writings today.

Joseph P. Free and Howard F. Vos say, "There are numerous works of the church fathers of the first and second centuries that speak in great detail of the reality of the Christ. And the New Testament, now recognized to be a first-century document, must be accepted as a reliable witness to Jesus' historicity."[50]

JESUS IS ETERNAL

In Revelation 21:6, Jesus says he lives forever. He said, "I am the Alpha and the Omega, the First and the Last. I am the Beginning and the End."

DID YOU KNOW?

• Jerusalem is a very important city. The Bible says that Jerusalem is the "apple of God's eye."[51] This means Jerusalem is very special to God. God will bless everyone who loves Jerusalem. He will destroy those who try to destroy the city or her people. Jerusalem will be the place Jesus will sit on his throne forever.

• Many Bible scholars agree that Jesus fulfilled four of the seven Jewish feasts. They look to future events described in the book of Revelation when Jesus will fulfill the final three feasts.

Seven Jewish Feasts

Passover: Celebrates how God delivered the Jews from the death of the firstborn son in Egypt by the blood of the Passover lamb. On this feast, Jesus was sacrificed as the Passover Lamb who delivers us from eternal death.

Unleavened Bread: Celebrates how Jews escaped so quickly from Egypt that their bread did not have time to rise. Unleavened bread is pierced and baked with stripes on it. On this feast, Jesus was whipped and stripes formed on his back. His side was pierced with a Roman sword.

Firstfruits: Celebrates the spring barley harvest. The first fruits of the harvest are given as an offering. Jesus rose from the grave on this feast and became the first to conquer death.

Pentecost (or Weeks): Celebrates the end of harvest. Remembers when God gave the Ten Commandments. Jesus gave the power of the Holy Spirit on this feast.

Feast of Trumpets (or Rosh Hashanah): Holy day announced with trumpet blasts. Jesus will appear with the blast of a trumpet to gather his church in the air. Another trumpet blast will announce his Second Coming.

Day of Atonement (or Yom Kippur): Each year the High Priest gave a special sacrifice to provide for forgiveness of sins. In the future, Jesus will have a special ceremony with the Jews who believe he is the Messiah. This will show how Jesus is the High Priest who died as the sacrifice for sins.

Booths: Celebrates the final harvest by building booths covered with branches and leaves. Remembers how God was with Moses and the Jews in the wilderness. In the future, Jesus will come back to rule for 1,000 years. All nations will come to Jerusalem to celebrate this feast with Jesus.

TIMELINE OF JESUS

(some dates are approximate)

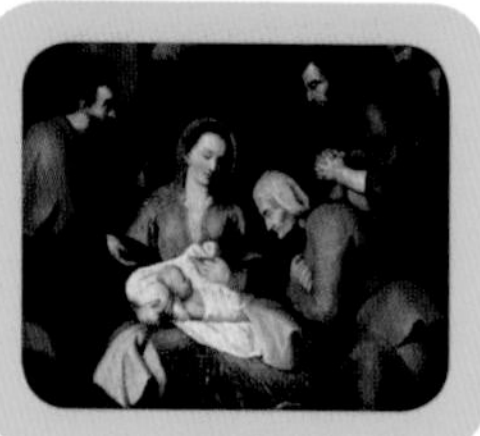
© Wikimedia Commons

4 BC
Jesus is born

© Wikimedia Commons

26 BC
Jesus is baptized

© Wikimedia Commons

8 AD
Jesus goes to temple when he is 12

© V. J. Matthew/Shutterstock

28 AD
Jesus chooses 12 disciples

WORLD HISTORY

31 BC–14 AD
Emperor Caesar Augustus

4 BC
Herod the Great dies

14 AD– 37 AD
Emperor Tiberius

25 AD
Western Han Dynasty ends in China

28 AD
Jesus preaches the "Sermon on the Mount"

30 AD
Jesus dies on the cross and comes to life again

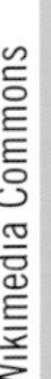

29 AD
Jesus heals the blind man

30 AD
Jesus appears to followers then goes up to heaven

26 AD–36 AD
Pilate governs Judea

43 AD
London founded

GLOSSARY

Aramaic: The language spoken by many Jews including Jesus

Baptize: A symbol of being washed clean from sin through faith in God

Chief priests: A group of official Jewish leaders

Christ: Greek word for "Messiah"

Christians: People who believe in Jesus Christ and his teachings

Cross: Two pieces of wood put together in the shape of a T that Romans used to kill criminals by hanging them on it

Essenes: Jewish group who wrote the Dead Sea Scrolls

Exodus: The escape of the Jews from Egypt

Eyewitness: Person who actually saw something happen

Feasts: Important holidays celebrated by the Jews

Forgive: To erase the record of sins

Garden of Gethsemane: A garden near Jerusalem

Good News: The news that Jesus is the Messiah, the Christ

Gospel: "Good news," each of the first four books of the New Testament

Greek: The language of the New Testament

Hebrews: Another name for Jews
High priest: The leader of all the priests
Holy Spirit: The Spirit of God
Hosanna: Word meaning "save"
I am: A special name for God meaning he is alive forever
Judgment: To make a decision, often between good and evil
Kingdom of heaven: The time in history when people believe Jesus is God
Law of Moses: The first five books in the Bible; includes the Ten Commandments
Messiah: The promised deliverer of the Jews
Miracles: Amazing events that only God can do
Parables: Simple stories that teach important lessons
Passover: A spring Jewish holiday when the Exodus is remembered
Persecution: Hurting or killing people because of their beliefs
Pharisees: Jewish group who followed traditions they made up
Priest: Person who performs important ceremonies of faith
Prophets: People who tell God's words to others
Repent: To turn away from sins and turn toward God

Sabbath: A special day of rest from Friday night to Saturday night

Sacrifice: A special gift to God such as an animal or grain

Sadducees: Jewish group who was strict about following God's Law, but did not follow the traditions of the Pharisees

Salvation: Saving from punishment

Sanhedrin: The highest group of Jewish leaders who met in Jerusalem and made important decisions

Satan: The devil

Savior: The One who saves people

Scribes: Scholars who study the Scriptures and copy them by hand

Sin: Bad things people think, say, or do

Son of God: A title for Jesus meaning he is the Messiah

Son of Man: A title Jesus used to show that even though he was God, he had come to earth as a man

Synagogue: Building where Jews meet for worship

Twelve Disciples: A special group of Jesus' closest followers

Wise Men: Scholars from Persia who gave gifts to Jesus

SELECTED BIBLIOGRAPHY

Alexander, David and Pat. *Zondervan Handbook to the Bible.* Grand Rapids, Michigan: Zondervan, 2002.

"Antiquities of the Jews," *The Works of Flavius Josephus,* December 21, 2013,

http://www.sacred-texts.com/jud/josephus/index.htm.

Burge, Gary M. *Jesus and the Jewish Festivals.* Grand Rapids, Michigan: Zondervan, 2012.

Campbell, Charlie H. Archaeological Evidence for the Bible: Exciting Discoveries Verifying Persons, Places and Events in the Bible. Carlsbad, California: The Always Be Ready Apologetics Ministry, 2012.

Campbell, Charlie H. *One Minute Answers to Skeptics' Top Forty Questions.* United States: Aquintas Publishing, 2005.

Connelly, Douglas. Amazing Discoveries that Unlock the Bible: A Visual Experience. Grand Rapids, Michigan: Zondervan, 2008.

Free, Joseph P. and Howard F. Vos. *Archaeology and Bible History.* Grand Rapids, Michigan: Zondervan, 1992.

Gardner, Paul D. *New International Encyclopedia of Bible Characters.* Grand Rapids, Michigan: Zondervan, 1995.

Gower, Ralph. The New Manners and Customs of Bible Times. Chicago: Moody Press, 1987.

Hindson, Ed. *Bible Prophecy from A to Z.* Forest, Virginia: The King is Coming College, 2012.

Hindson, Ed. *Understanding Revelation in One Hour.* Colton, California: The King is Coming Telecast, 2011.

House, H. Wayne. Zondervan Charts: Chronological and Background Charts of the New Testament. Grand Rapids: Michigan, 2009.

Matthews, Victor H. *Manners and Customs in the Bible.* Peabody, Massachusetts: Hendrickson Publishers, 1991.

Missler, Chuck. *Learn the Bible in 24 Hours.* Nashville: Thomas Nelson Publishers, 2002.

Rasmussen, Carl G. *Zondervan Atlas of the Bible.* Grand Rapids: Zondervan, 2010.

Silva, Moisé and J.D. Douglas and Merrill C. Tenney. *Zondervan Illustrated Bible Dictionary.* Grand Rapids, Michigan: Zondervan, 2011.

Strobel, Lee. *The Case for the Resurrection.* Grand Rapids, Michigan: Zondervan, 2009.

Tenney, Merrill C., General Editor. *The Zondervan Encyclopedia of the Bible, Volumes 1–5.* Grand Rapids, Michigan: Zondervan, 2009.

"The Annals by Tacitus, Book XV," *The Annals by Tacitus,* March 22, 2013, http://classics.mit.edu/Tacitus/annals.11.xv.html.

"The Wars of the Jews," *The Works of Flavius Josephus,* April 6, 2013, http://www.sacred-texts.com/jud/josephus/index.htm.

Throckmorton, Burton H. Jr. *Gospel Parallels: A Synopsis of the First Three Gospels.* Nashville: Thomas Nelson Publishers, 1979.

Vos, Howard F. *Nelson's New Illustrated Bible Manners & Customs.* Nashville: Thomas Nelson, 1999.

Walton, John H., Mark L. Strauss, and Ted Cooper Jr. *The Essential Bible Companion.* Grand Rapids, Michigan: Zondervan, 2006.

SOURCE NOTES

1. Caption (and quote in caption) from source: Campbell, Charlie H. *Archaeological Evidence for the Bible: Exciting Discoveries Verifying Persons, Places and events in the Bible.* Carlsbad, California: The Always Be Ready Apologetics Ministry, 2012, pages 118–119.

2. Campbell, Charlie H. *Archaeological Evidence for the Bible: Exciting Discoveries Verifying Persons, Places and events in the Bible.* Carlsbad, California: The Always Be Ready Apologetics Ministry, 2012, page 14.

3. Exodus 20, NIrV

4. Luke 1:31, NIrV

5. Luke 2:10–11, NIrV

6. Luke 2:30, NIrV

7. "Antiquities of the Jews, 18.3.3," *The Works of Flavius Josephus,* December 21, 2013, http://www.sacred-texts.com/jud/josephus/index.htm.

8. "Wars of the Jews, 1.21.1," *The Works of Flavius Josephus,* December 21, 2013, http://www.sacred-texts.com/jud/josephus/index.htm.

9. Matthew 3:15, NIrV

10. Matthew 3:17, NIrV

11. Matthew 4:17, NIrV

12. Matthew 18:5, NIrV

13. Matthew 18:6, NIrV

14. "Antiquities of the Jews, 18.5.2," *The Works of Flavius*

Josephus, December 21, 2013, http://www.sacred-texts.com/jud/josephus/index.htm.

15. Matthew 22:29, NIrV

16. Campbell, Charlie H. *One Minute Answers to Skeptics' Top Forty Questions.* United States: Aquintas Publishing, 2005, page 30.

17. Mark 2:5, NIrV

18. Mark 2:6, NIrV

19. John 8:57, NIrV

20. John 8:58, NIrV

21. Mark 3:21, NIrV

22. John 4:42, NIrV

23. Matthew 16:15, NIrV

24. Matthew 16:16, NIrV

25. Matthew 16:17, NIrV

26. John 9:11–12, NIrV

27. John 9:32–33, NIrV

28. John 9:38, NIrV

29. Matthew 9:35, NIrV

30. John 11:47–48, NIrV

31. Matthew 20:18–19, NIrV

32. Matthew 26:10–12, NIrV

33. John 12:13, NIrV

34. Matthew 21:13, NIrV

35. Matthew 26:39, NIrV

36. Mark 14:36, NIrV

37. Mark 14:41–42, NIrV

38. Zechariah 9:9, NIrV

39. Matthew 26:56, NIrV

40. Mark 14:61–62, NIrV

41. Matthew 27:37, NIrV

42. Luke 23:46, NIrV

43. Mark 15:39, NIrV

44. "The Annals by Tacitus, Book XV," *The Annals by Tacitus*, March 22, 2013, http://classics.mit.edu/Tacitus/annals.11.xv.html.

45. Matthew 27:63–65, NIrV

46. "The Wars of the Jews, 4.5.2," *The Works of Flavius Josephus*, April 6, 2013, http://www.sacred-texts.com/jud/josephus/war – 4.htm.

47. John 20:17, NIrV

48. John 20:22, NIrV

49. Acts 1:6, NIrV

50. Free, Joseph P. and Howard F. Vos. *Archaeology and Bible History.* Grand Rapids, Michigan: Zondervan, 1992, page 244.

51. Zechariah 2:8, NKJV

STUDENT RESOURCES

Blankenbaker, Frances. *What the Bible Is All About for Young Explorers*. Ventura, California: Regal Books, 1986.

Dowley, Tim. *The Student Bible Atlas*. Minneapolis: Augsburg, 1996.

Ham, Ken with Cindy Malott, *The Answers Book for Kids, Volume 1: 22 Questions from Kids on Creation and the Fall*. Green Forest, Arizona: Master Books, 2008.

Ham, Ken with Cindy Malott, *The Answers Book for Kids, Volume 3: 22 Questions from Kids on God and the Bible*. Green Forest, Arizona: Master Books, 2009.

Ham, Ken with Cindy Malott, *The Answers Book for Kids, Volume 4: 22 Questions from Kids on Sin, Salvation, and the Christian Life*. Green Forest, Arizona: Master Books, 2009.

McDowell, Josh and Sean McDowell. *Jesus is Alive! Evidence for the Resurrection for Kids*. Ventura, California: Regal, 2009.

Osborne, Rick and K. Christie Bowler. *I Want to Know About God, Jesus, the Bible, and Prayer*. Grand Rapids, Michigan: Zonderkidz, 2000.

Strobel, Lee with Rob Suggs and Robert Elmer. *Case for Christ for Kids*. Grand Rapids, Michigan: Zonderkidz, 2010.

Van der Maas, Ruth, Marnie Wooding, and Rick Osborne. *Kid Atlas: Important Places in the Bible and Where to Find Them*. Grand Rapids, Michigan: Zonderkidz, 2002.

Water, Mark. *The Big Book About Jesus*. Nashville: Thomas Nelson Publishers, 1995.

Water, Mark. *The Big Book of Bible People*. Nashville: Thomas Nelson Publishers, 1996.

Water, Mark. *The Children's Bible Encyclopedia*. Owing Mills, Maryland: Baker, 1998.

Water, Mark. *The Children's Encyclopedia of Bible Times*. Grand Rapids, Michigan: Zondervan Publishing House, 1995.

ABOUT THE AUTHOR

Nancy I. Sanders is the bestselling children's author of over 80 books including *Old Testament Days: An Activity Guide* with over 80 hands-on projects. Her award-winning nonfiction children's books include *D is for Drinking Gourd: An African American Alphabet, America's Black Founders,* and *Frederick Douglass for Kids*. Nancy delights in making history come alive for young readers. She lives with her husband, Jeff, and their two cats in sunny southern California. Nancy and Jeff have two grown sons, Dan and Ben (with his lovely wife Christina). Visit Nancy's website at www.nancyisanders.com.

Mary

Get to Know Series

Nancy I. Sanders

Mary—part of the Get to Know series—will teach you everything you need to know about this young woman whom God used to do great things! Mary was more than the mother of Jesus. She was a hero of the Bible. She said "Yes!" to God. Learn about Mary and her exciting place in history. Discover what it was like to grow up in Israel and be a part of Jesus' life on earth.

Featuring a bibliography and scriptural references throughout, this is sure to become a favorite for young readers and for first book reports.

Available in stores and online!

King David

Get to Know Series

Nancy I. Sanders

King David—part of the Get to Know series—will teach you everything you need to know about an imperfect young man whom God used to do great things! David lived an adventurous life. He protected his family's sheep from lions and bears. He fought a giant with just a sling and stone. He even spent years hiding from men who were trying to kill him. And eventually, David became a great king. But David was also a man of God. Learn more about this hero from the Bible and his exciting place in history. Discover what it was like to grow up in ancient Israel and then be a king of God's people.

Featuring a bibliography and scriptural references throughout, this is sure to become a favorite for young readers and for first book reports.

Available in stores and online!

Apostle Paul

Get to Know Series

Nancy I. Sanders

Apostle Paul—part of the Get to Know series—is a unique biography about Paul. Focusing on the life and character of this Biblical hero, using color photographs, maps, and other visual resources to tell the whole story, young biography fans will come to learn more about this man of the God, his writings, his impact on the early church, and the role he plays in history.

Featuring a bibliography and scriptural references throughout, this is sure to become a favorite for young readers and for first book reports.